The Peace Book

TODD PARR

Megan Tingley Books

LITTLE, BROWN AND COMPANY

New York   Boston

This book is dedicated to the world.
Love,
Todd

Little, Brown and Company

Hachette Book Group
1290 Avenue of the Americas
New York, NY 10104
Visit our website at www.lb-kids.com

Little, Brown and Company is a division of Hachette Book Group, Inc.
The Little, Brown name and logo are trademarks of Hachette Book Group, Inc.

The publisher is not responsible for websites (or their content) that are not owned by the publisher.

First Paperback Edition: April 2009
Originally published in hardcover in September 2004 by Little, Brown and Company

Library of Congress Cataloging-in-Publication Data

Parr, Todd.
    The peace book / Todd Parr.—1st ed.
        p. cm.
"Megan Tingley Books."
Summary: Describes peace as making new friends, sharing a meal, feeling good about yourself, and more.
    [1. Peace—Fiction.] I. Title
PZ7.P2447 Pe 2003
[E]—dc22   2003058914
ISBN 978-0-316-04349-6 (pb) / ISBN 978-0-316-83531-2 (hc 10x10) / ISBN 978-0-316-05962-6 (hc 9x9)

10 9

IM

Printed in China

Peace is making new friends

Peace is keeping the water blue for all the fish

Peace is listening to different kinds of music

Peace is saying you're sorry when you hurt someone

Peace is helping your neighbor

Peace is reading all different kinds of books

Peace is thinking about
someone you love

Peace is giving shoes to

someone who needs them

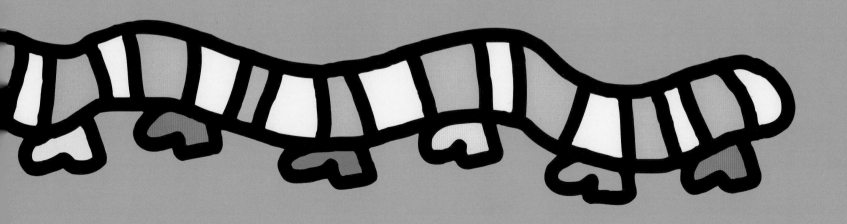

Peace is planting a tree

Peace is sharing a meal

Peace is wearing different clothes

Peace is watching it snow

Peace is keeping the streets clean

Peace is offering a hug
to a friend

having a home

Dog

Peace is growing a garden

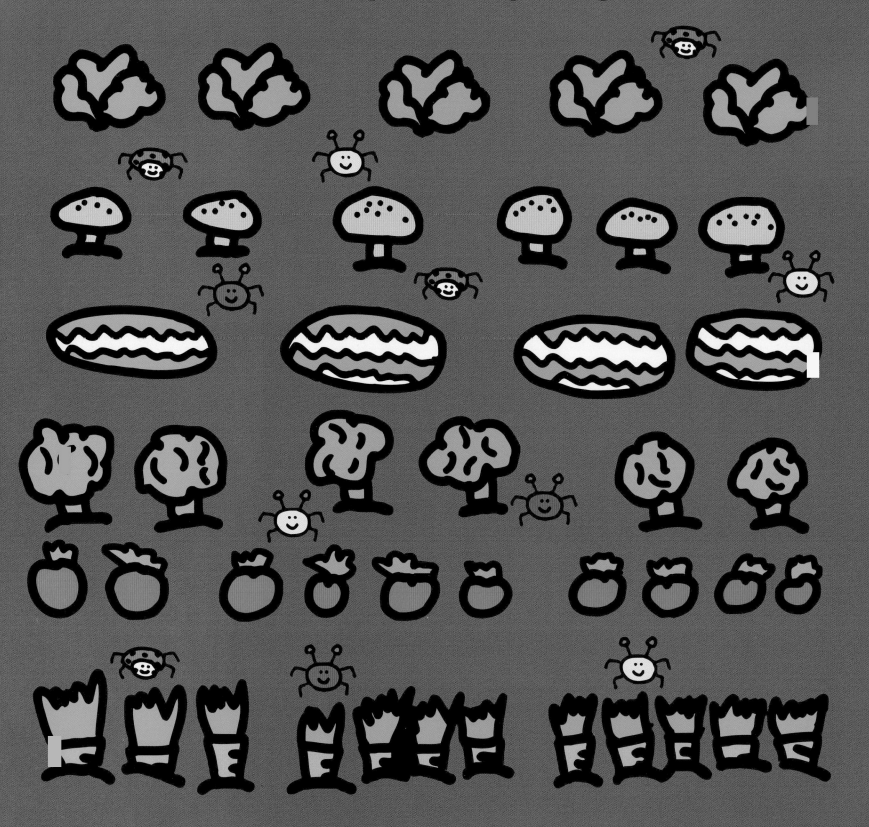

Peace is taking a nap

Peace is learning another language

Peace is having enough pizza in the world for everyone

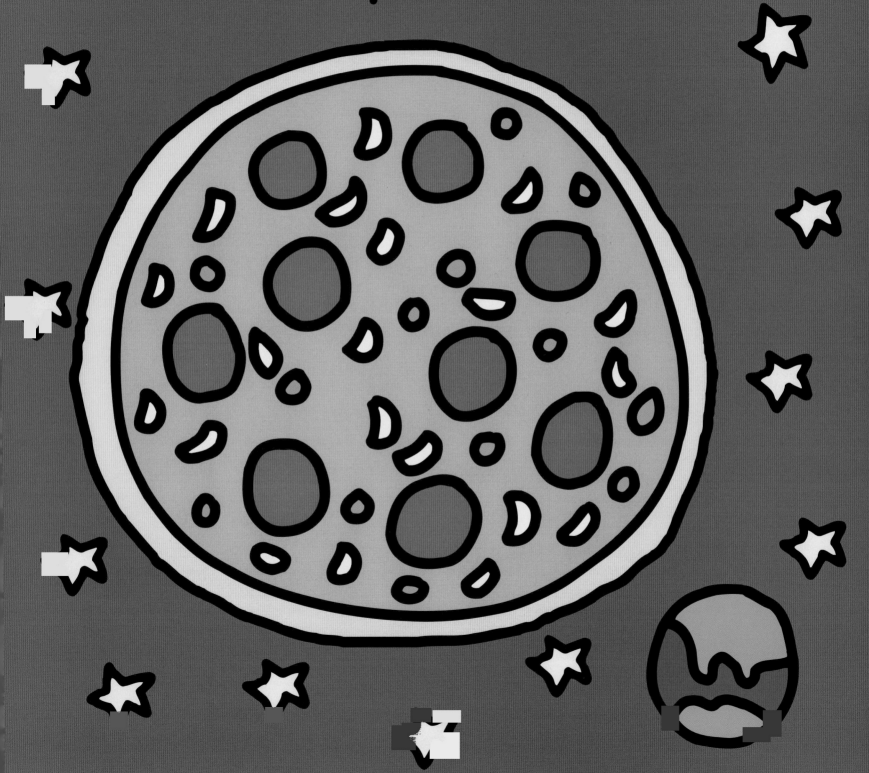

Peace is keeping someone warm

Peace is new babies being born

Peace is being free

Peace is traveling to different places

Peace is wishing on a star

who you are

PEACE 🐦 is being different, feeling good about yourself, and helping others. The world 🌍 is a better place because of YOU!

♥ Love, Todd